medicine women

paintings *by* PATRICIA WYATT
text *by* SUSAN FREILICHER

POMEGRANATE ARTBOOKS
san francisco

Great Spirit, I thank you for this moment, for my life, for allowing me to hear the people in my paintings. I ask that you hear my prayers today and know that they come from the purest of intentions and from the love in my heart.

I ask that you hear the prayers of women who are born today, who die today, who give birth today, who bury a child today, who have their first menstruation today, who never menstruate after today, who paint, who write, who sing, who teach, who dance, who love—please hear what is in the hearts of *all* Medicine Women.

I ask that you hear my prayer for my child Theo, who honored my choices before even I could, that he remain on his path with an open heart.

Mitakuye Oyasin
For All My Relations,
Patricia Wyatt
Tesuque, New Mexico
August 1993

In the beginning there was a dream and a vision. So we smoked the pipe and let our prayers rise with the smoke for the Great Spirit to hear. And Spirit heard and Spirit answered.

This book is a collaboration between artist and writer, business partners, sisters in the light, two women on the Medicine Path and most of all friends. The writings were done after meditations on each painting. It is the Medicine Beings, be they four-leggeds, two-leggeds or winged ones, that are giving us these gifts.

These writings are dedicated to the memory of my father, who believed I could accomplish anything I set my mind to, and to my mother, whose continuing encouragement and support have enabled me to do so.

Susan Freilicher
Santa Fe, New Mexico
August 1993

medicine women
Paintings by Patricia Wyatt
Text by Susan Freilicher

Published by Pomegranate Artbooks
Box 6099, Rohnert Park, California 94927

ISBN 1-56640-598-X
Library of Congress Catalog Card Number 93-84776

Printed in Korea

contents

introduction

For as long as there has been time, there have been Medicine Women. They have worn different faces, taken different forms, spoken many tongues and been called by numerous names: midwife, witch, priestess, warrior, herbalist, nurse, doctor, sister, wife, friend, lover, mother and *woman,* all the women who have walked the Medicine Path. For many centuries we did not see Medicine Woman. She hid in fear behind the mask of complacency. She was suppressed under the feet of patriarchy. Today, slowly, she is beginning to show her face again.

In Native American tradition a person's medicine is that which brings her power, teaches lessons and in turn empowers. Medicine Women are dispensers of power, instruments of healing, keepers of tradition and teachers to us all. Some Medicine Women are trained through formal education while others apprentice with elders. Many others turn inward and follow the innate instincts of the feminine—to nurture, to create, to heal.

Every day we encounter Medicine Woman. She is the mother comforting a child. She is the teacher in front of the classroom. She is the midwife bringing forth new life. She is the nurse holding the hand of the sick and dying. She is the painter, the writer, the musician, the poet. She stands on the picket lines and behind sales counters. She is the stranger who shares a smile. She is your friend who cheers you on. She is the part of you that knows you can. There is powerful medicine in us all. The Medicine Woman encourages others to be their best, to honor their own choices.

Several years ago, Patricia Wyatt began a new series of paintings. "These People," as she would refer to them, started appearing in her work. Images, symbols, tapestries of a time gone by. Images and symbols that were not in her everyday consciousness. People who viewed the work began to sense and be affected by the immense power they held. One day one of her teachers asked how long she had been painting "the ancient ones." The Medicine Women and Men were showing their faces through Patricia's art.

We are drawing the curtain on not only this century but this millennium. The world has never been so far advanced and yet so backward. The same advances that take us to the moon and stars have left us disconnected from the Earth Mother. People are on a new search for their personal truths and a simpler way of life. Through the paintings of Patricia Wyatt, we can see the messengers and learn the message of those who have returned to help us. The Medicine Women in these paintings bear us gifts. These gifts help us heal ourselves; our four-legged relations; our winged relations; our relations that swim in the waters and that crawl on the earth; the plant, rock and tree relations; and the relationship we have to our Planet, our Mother.

peacemaker is
surrounded by doves
and her generous heart
is illuminated
by the moon

Until we let peace into our own lives, we cannot expect the world to live in peace. If we cannot keep peace in our homes, our families, our jobs, our schools, our neighborhoods, our towns, our cities, our countries, then what hope does the world have for peace?

Peacemaker Is Surrounded by Doves and Her Generous Heart Is Illuminated by the Moon, 1990.
Watercolor, color pencil and oil pastel, 50 x 60 in.

reflections of
her heart

The good red road of life leads from mother to daughter
and to her daughter in turn—and to all the generations
of daughters. It is the way of grandmother and maiden,
of mother and child, of woman in all her many phases.
It is the path that leads to the *Reflections of Her Heart*.

Reflections of Her Heart, 1993.
Watercolor, color pencil and oil pastel, 32 x 40 in.

mountain lion is her ally

Silently they prowl, hunting in the darkness of the night, killing only what they need to survive. Alone they walk, in the mountains and wilderness caves. Now they hide from people, their most dangerous predators.

Mountain lion medicine surrounds this beautiful princess. She has learned the power of silence and understands the quest to survive.

Mountain Lion Is Her Ally, 1990.
Watercolor, color pencil and oil pastel, 60 x 40 in.

crimson daughter
of ancient people

We are all *Crimson Daughter of Ancient People,* though our eyes may be blue or green and our hair is no longer the color of raven wings.

On the cliffs of ancient dwellings we've stood and offered prayers to the gods.

Our feet have danced and our hearts have beat to the rhythm of the drums.

Our blood has raced at the sight of our man, and our hearts have bled at the loss of a child.

We are the daughters of generations who were white and brown and yellow and red. We are Hindu and Christian and Jew and Pagan and Buddhist and Muslim and more.

We are all *Crimson Daughter of Ancient People.*

Crimson Daughter of Ancient People, 1989.
Watercolor, color pencil and oil pastel, 30 x 50 in.

the elders are above, below and alongside us

Western society thinks linearly. The theory of evolution starts with the amoeba and works its way up. Our wisdom is judged by degrees and years. If you live long enough you become an elder, and by the very fact of your age you are expected to know.

Is it wisdom or arrogance that makes us believe this? Can we learn any less from an earthworm than from an octogenarian?

The Elders Are Above, Below and Alongside Us, 1991.
Watercolor, color pencil and oil pastel, 40 x 46 in.

14

her heart can make a slow bud open

A beautiful woman can inspire songs, poetry and gifts of precious jewels. But the medicine of an open and loving heart can inspire a flower bud to bloom and share its beauty with the world.

Her Heart Can Make a Slow Bud Open, 1988.
Watercolor, color pencil and oil pastel, 45 x 35 in.

the wedding song

This young man and woman have donned their finest robes to celebrate their wedding. She gazes lovingly at him as they begin their marriage journey. They enter this day with the intention of living life together.

The Wedding Song brings us the medicine of commitment. Commitment begins with ourselves and then moves to others in our lives, our community, our country and our planet.

The Wedding Song, 1990.
Watercolor, color pencil and oil pastel, 50 x 60 in.

hawk whispers his message of awareness

She takes one last look back before she continues her journey. Above her *Hawk Whispers His Message of Awareness*. He flies high and sees clearly. He does not flinch at the unpleasantries of life but watches and stays out of harm's way.

Though we walk the Mother and don't fly the skies, we can heed hawk's message. It brings us the medicine of awareness of our surroundings.

Hawk Whispers His Message of Awareness, 1993.
Watercolor, color pencil and oil pastel, 32 x 40 in.

elements of spirit

A tapestry, a man, a woman, the cactus in the desert, a feather headdress: all are *Elements of Spirit*. They show us that spirit is everywhere and in everything.

Elements of Spirit, 1989.
Watercolor, color pencil and oil pastel, 60 x 40 in.

morning light reveals her change

She greets the dawn with dragonflies to hear her prayers.

When problems weigh heavily on our minds and hearts, the night can seem endless. Troubles seem magnified, and shadows of familiar objects take on nightmarish proportions. As the sun rises in the east, cracks of light break the darkness of the sky just as cracks of hope break the solitude of the night.

Morning Light Reveals Her Change, 1990.
Watercolor, color pencil and oil pastel, 60 x 40 in.

patterns weave the search to spirit end

Their search is a lifelong journey. The patterns of their lives are woven by the wind as they walk together, seeking the wisdom of spirit.

Patterns Weave the Search to Spirit End, 1989.
Watercolor, color pencil and oil pastel, 40 x 60 in.

the red road leads home

Here stands a warrior in her knowing. She follows the path she's known for generations: *The Red Road Leads Home.*

The Red Road Leads Home, 1992.
Watercolor, color pencil and oil pastel, 40 x 60 in.

blanket spirits

What messages and stories are entwined in the symbols
and colors that, woven together, became a blanket?

Blanket Spirits, 1989.
Watercolor, color pencil and oil pastel, 40 x 30 in.

Dreamwalker's heart is in the south

As we walk the Medicine Wheel of our lives, we travel from the east to the south. The south is the summer of our lives—the time when we come of age, when we play, laze in the heat of the sun, savor the longness of the day, become intoxicated by a flower's perfume, read the message written in the stars and feel the heat of our passions.

Dreamwalker's Heart Is in the South brings the medicine of passion and creativity into our lives. She asks us to remember when our lives held promise and passion, when life was so exciting that our hearts beat like the pounding of horses' hooves. She dares us to expect our dreams and fantasies to become reality. She brings us the medicine of our own potential.

Dreamwalker's Heart Is in the South, 1992.
Watercolor, color pencil and oil pastel, 40 x 60 in.

swan's reflection

A swan glides across the lake, its movements too subtle to disturb its reflection in the water.

Swan's Reflection portrays a man and a woman standing side by side on the journey of life. They are surrounded by swans gliding by, showing their reflections. This man and this woman, like the swans that surround them, reflect themselves in each other.

Swan's Reflection, 1990.
Watercolor, color pencil and oil pastel, 50 x 60 in.

medicine people

The ancient *Medicine People* wore animal robes and put feathers in their hair. Their medicine bags were sacred, carrying totems and symbols of their personal medicine.

Medicine People, 1992.
Watercolor, color pencil and oil pastel, 30 x 60 in.

grey hawk dreamer

In the darkness she comes to fly us all away to her dreamtime. Hers is the medicine of perspective: she knows that life is not black and white, but many shades of grey.

Grey Hawk Dreamer, 1989.
Watercolor, color pencil and oil pastel, 60 x 40 in.

shadows of forgotten ancestors

I stand on the bluff and watch the buffalo graze below.

I am Lakota, Ute, Arapaho, Shoshone, Chippewa, Cheyenne.

I leave the woods and walk to the shore to watch the gulls drop clams on the rocks.

I am Micmac, Algonquin, Pequot, Delaware, Iroquois, Shinnecock.

I carve a hole in the ice and pray for the fish to come to our lines.

I am Aleut, Ingalik, Tanaina, Tlingit.

I climb out of the kiva from the depths of the darkness to the turquoise of the sky.

I am Hopi, Zuni, Tesuque, Cochiti, San Ildefonso.

Shadows of Forgotten Ancestors, 1990.
Watercolor, color pencil and oil pastel, 40 x 60 in.

for all my relations

To honor and respect every rock and plant and living creature as you would your own god is to know the medicine of *For All My Relations*.

For All My Relations, 1992.
Watercolor, color pencil and oil pastel, 50 x 60 in.

her message comes from the thunder beings

Her message—insight—bursts into awareness like the sound of thunder beings gathering over the mountains on a summer night. The powerful voice of the thunder beings commands her attention and teaches her to listen even in the silence.

Her Message Comes from the Thunder Beings, 1989.
Watercolor, color pencil and oil pastel, 45 x 48 in.

she dreams in the rhythm of the waves

From the depths of the waters emerges a beautiful woman. Her hair and blankets flow like the waters and tides from which she emerged.

She Dreams in the Rhythm of the Waves brings us the medicine of the tides. She teaches us to flow with the rhythm of our lives. The dolphins on her blanket lead us on the journey of cooperation with each other and with the world around us.

She Dreams in the Rhythm of the Waves, 1990.
Watercolor, color pencil and oil pastel, 60 x 30 in.

servants for the valley

These beautiful Pueblo women begin their days in peace and composure. They remember what many have forgotten: to be of service and to perform that service with dignity is to truly be holy. Theirs is the medicine of unconditional love. It is dedicated to anyone who has helped someone in need, cared for the sick, fought a fire, defended a life, voiced a protest, given freely of herself.

Servants for the Valley, 1989.
Watercolor, color pencil and oil pastel, 40 x 60 in.

embraced by spirit

Embraced by Spirit is composed as the geese fly by.
Brother wind unfolds her hair and sister butterfly alights
on her blanket. She brings the medicine of stillness.

Embraced by Spirit, 1991.
Watercolor, color pencil and oil pastel, 52 x 30 in.

mind, body and spirit medicine being shared

Are we flesh and blood only?

How do you measure the strength of a soul?

Is the woman the wolf or the wolf the woman?

In the separation we are lost.

Mind, Body and Spirit Medicine Being Shared, 1992.
Watercolor, color pencil and oil pastel, 30 x 60 in.

she walked before us

She Walked Before Us brings us the medicine of determination, which helps us get where we are going and leave when it is time to go.

She Walked Before Us, 1992.
Watercolor, color pencil and oil pastel, 40 x 45 in.

keepers of the dream lodge

The women and the wolf stand guard at the gates of twilight. By the fullness of the moon they hold their vigil, protecting the medicine of dreams.

Keepers of the Dream Lodge, 1990.
Watercolor, color pencil and oil pastel, 50 x 60 in.

the gentle winds of the east wrap this blanket around her

The sun rises in the east and brings the yellow light of dawn to sleeping peoples. The east is the spring of our lives, when butterflies float on the air and the world is fertile with new life.

The medicine brought by the east winds is the gift of vision and enlightenment.

The Gentle Winds of the East Wrap This Blanket Around Her, 1991.
Watercolor, color pencil and oil pastel, 50 x 35 in.

this granddaughter is guided by the wisdom of the grandmothers

With love in her eyes and trust in her heart she listens for the guidance of the grandmothers. Theirs is the medicine of openness and receptivity. She hears her name called by the grandmother winds and sees it written in the smiling face of grandmother moon.

This Granddaughter Is Guided by the Wisdom of the Grandmothers, 1991.
Watercolor, color pencil and oil pastel, 30 x 40 in.

colors of wind

Colors of Wind walks the path of beauty. She stands with her feather fan ready to smudge and bless those who cross her path. She walks against a backdrop of yellows and oranges and reds that are both the sunrises and the sunsets of our lives.

The medicine she brings is that of the wind. When the wind blows it creates change—calm waters ripple, leaves flutter and change colors and love songs play where once there was silence. *Colors of Wind* allows us to see the wind and the change.

Colors of Wind, 1988.
Watercolor, color pencil and oil pastel, 40 x 50 in.

her secret is in the land

A beautiful woman stands alone against a mesa-silhouetted sky. Even the brilliance of the sun cannot outshine her radiance. With composed dignity she gazes down to the earth. What does she see? What does she know?

Her Secret Is in the Land, 1993.
Watercolor, color pencil and oil pastel, 32 x 40 in.

new moon vision quest

New Moon Vision Quest stands against a dark sky with only her bright robes lending color to the night and her bear allies for companionship.

The new moon is the darkest of nights and the end of the moon cycle. In our lives the new moon symbolizes a time of rest, old age and the wisdom of the crone. It provides time for us to rewrite the story of our lives on the blank slate of the sky.

New Moon Vision Quest, 1992.
Watercolor, color pencil and oil pastel, 45 x 41 in.

hummingbirds are her allies

She sits on her throne holding a royal scepter fan. Her subjects hover close by. The hummingbirds are among the smallest of their kind, yet there is an endurance and flexibility to their flight.

Some myths claim hummingbirds got their bright colors by traveling too close to the sun. Others say they were messengers to the underworld. Hummingbird medicine can teach us to fly to our heights or reach down to the depths of our own personal underworlds.

Hummingbirds Are Her Allies, 1991.
Watercolor, color pencil and oil pastel, 50 x 60 in.

her spirit is as gentle as butterfly

As they whisper in the wind the butterflies surround her spirit and guide her soul. Butterflies bring the medicine of transformation. They begin their lives crawling on their bellies. At the cocoon stage they wrap themselves in a protective layer of introspection. Then they transform themselves into symbols of light and ethereal beauty as they spread their painted wings across the air.

Her Spirit Is as Gentle as Butterfly, 1992.
Watercolor, color pencil and oil pastel, 60 x 31 in.

she surrenders in grace

She lifts her face to the morning sun, trusting that it will warm her. She raises her arms to the afternoon winds, knowing that they will transport her. She opens her heart to the birds winging across the sky, understanding that they are her sisters. *She Surrenders in Grace.*

She Surrenders in Grace, 1990.
Watercolor, color pencil and oil pastel, 60 x 35 in.

their shadows
seek each other

A Pueblo man and woman are drawn together, but they cannot look at each other. It is not from the light but from their shadows that they seek each other's comfort.

Their Shadows Seek Each Other, 1992.
Watercolor, color pencil and oil pastel, 35 x 55 in.

lightning ignites inspiration

Inspiration is the foundation of creation. It comes in many forms: sunrises, sunsets, moonlight, starlight, mountains, deserts, forests, oceans and streams. First loves, last kisses, hometowns, holidays and the end of days. Our inspiration to write, paint, sing, dance, play is all around.

Lightning Ignites Inspiration, 1993.
Watercolor, color pencil and oil pastel, 38 x 45 in.

her soul is wolf

In her trust she allows us to see her soul and her personal medicine—wolf. With ghostly howling in the night sky, the wolves surround her. Her soul is wild and untamed, yet she needs the company of the pack and the companionship of a life mate to survive. *Her Soul Is Wolf* travels a difficult path, for hers is the medicine of vulnerability.

Her Soul Is Wolf, 1993.
Watercolor, color pencil and oil pastel, 32 x 40 in.

butterfly brings awaited change

Butterfly Brings Awaited Change alights on the throat of the bride. Just as the butterfly's wings flutter in the air, words of change can flutter around our throats until we send them out into the universe.

Butterfly Brings Awaited Change, 1993.
Watercolor, color pencil and oil pastel, 32 x 40 in.

she is cared for by mother earth

Amidst a garden of flowers with leaves growing up to Father Sky stands the warrior with sadness in her eyes. Her return is a reminder—*She Is Cared For by Mother Earth.*

She Is Cared For by Mother Earth, 1993.
Watercolor, color pencil and oil pastel, 32 x 40 in

they listen
to the silence

We are so bombarded with noise that we've forgotten how to listen to the silence. The medicine of silence speaks in the loudest voice of all.

They Listen to the Silence, 1989.
Watercolor, color pencil and oil pastel, 40 x 60 in.

spirit moon

Out of the caves we crawled to honor her majesty. In the deserts and forests, on the mountaintops and in the valleys, the peoples of the lands saw her face. They knew her then, her power, her essence, without explanation. Hers is the medicine of magic. She is the *Spirit Moon.*

Spirit Moon, 1993.
Watercolor, color pencil and oil pastel, 32 x 40 in.

mother earth's sister

In a universe where peace prevails she holds her vigil, eyes cast into the dark abyss of the night sky.

From the beginning there were always two, Mother Earth and her sister. Will there now be only one? Neither the rumbling of thunder nor the fall of rain describes the grief of *Mother Earth's Sister*.

Mother Earth's Sister, 1993.
Watercolor, color pencil and oil pastel, 32 x 40 in.

honoring the mother

She weeps for the Earth's wounds. Tenderly she cradles all the creatures of the land, all the growing things. She is *Honoring the Mother*.

Honoring the Mother, 1991.
Watercolor, color pencil and oil pastel, 60 x 40 in.

the landscape

Some say we evolved from primates, others that we are the descendants of lost civilizations. Still others claim we are children of the stars. Regardless of our origin, we are here. We have flourished.

And at last we are learning to cherish the Mother that has nourished us. Medicine Women, Men and Relations from all nations have given us prophecy: the Mother will survive.

The Landscape, 1993.
Watercolor, color pencil and oil pastel, 32 x 36 in.